Love Saved Me

A Collection of Poems on Love and Compassion

LUKE ROUKER

DEDICATION

To my wife,
For loving me so fiercely
That I stayed on this earth,
Even when the darkness whispered its temptations.
Your love anchored me,
A beacon in the storm that made me believe
There was still light to be found.

To my best friend,
Who has stood by my side, unwavering,
Your loyalty is a constant presence.
Thank you for shaping this book with your insight,
For your hand in the words I offer here.

To my parents,
For adopting me and showing me
Unconditional love from the very beginning.
Your support helped shape the man I've become.

To Christ Lutheran Church in Wise, Virginia,
You gave me my values,
The roots of compassion and kindness,
That still bloom within me.
And to First UU in Columbus, Ohio,
For being their continuation,
A space where those values found new life.

To every being I've come in contact with,
For your role in my journey,
Whether through kindness or hardship,
Each contribution has shaped me.
I would not be who I am without you all.

Love Saved Me

And finally,
To the person I have been, who wrote on those days,
When vulnerability was a fragile, trembling thing -
Thank you for being brave enough to feel.
I am honored to share your joys and sorrows in these pages,
Grateful to carry your voice forward,
For your story is still unfolding,
And I can't wait to see who we will become.

CONTENTS

ACKNOWLEDGMENTS

First, I want to thank my wife, Vanessa, for her consistent support and for reading my work. Your insights and encouragement helped shape this book in ways I could never have imagined.

To my best friend, Christian, thank you for not only reading and making suggestions that improved my writing but also for providing the beautiful cover art that brings this book to life. Your talent and friendship are a gift.

A special thanks to ChatGPT, my editor and collaborator, for working with me to refine and elevate these poems. Your input has been invaluable in making these words stronger.

Lastly, to you, the reader - thank you for giving this book a chance. Some of these poems may take you to difficult places, but I hope you'll stay with them long enough to find the light at the end. Your time and openness mean more to me than I can express.

2021
THESE POEMS ARE MY FIRST ENDEAVOR INTO
POETRY, WRITTEN IN MY BASEMENT AFTER
WORK.

Darkness

02/14/2021

The man who raised me has gone blind
The world he once knew,
   full of football players,
   grilled meats,
   and produce shelves
Is now a memory
Replaced by splotches of newscasters and partial phone
   numbers
A black splotch covers
   his wife's face,
   the score of the game,
   the price of a jug of milk,
   everything he most wants to see
If he lives to meet my children, he will only know their faces
   as splotches
His world gets darker every day, and we do our best to fill in
   the gaps
We read for him,
   type for him,
   make his meals,
   and set up his entertainments
We can never do enough to fill what the splotches have
   taken
I ask him every day, "Dad, how can I help?"
I am often met with silence, or a sad smile and simply, "I'm
   okay, thanks."
I wish I could do more for you, Dad.

Overwhelm

2021

I watch the white numbers in the corner of my screen blip to
  06:00

My heart sinks, my mind is full of To-Dos left undone, piling
  onto the heaping queue labeled only, "Tomorrow"

I softly shut the lid of the machine and start the stove.

I hear the beep of the alarm chirping into my consciousness.

My stomach grumbles, my hands burn on the edge of a pot
  too hot to grab.

I place my plate and fork in the sink, and descend to the
  basement.

Even here, I feel the pressure of the day.

Will I finish that project?

Can I please my boss?

What about my parents? My wife? Our dog?

Did I leave the stove on?

Will tomorrow be like today?

Endless Red

2021

The engineer gulps today's second cup of coffee.
His body asked for water, but the caffeine seems more
    important right now to his internal executive.
His machine barks out another Red error message,
    stubbornly doing precisely what he asked it to.
Over and over he gives the wrong commands.
His mind races,
"What if I can't finish in time?
What happens if I never get that red to turn green?
Am I a bad engineer?"
Red again.
The clock on his office wall ticks obnoxiously.
His hands poke the keys with force as if ordering the right
    string of characters to come out.
Red.
He swears under his breath.
His stomach gurgles.
His mouth feels dry.
Reluctantly, he gets up.
He uses the restroom,
    washes his hands,
    eats a snack,
    and drinks a cool glass of water.
He sits back down.
Quickly, he spots it.
The single line that ruined his day.
Suddenly, Green.

Next

2021

I know I need to do a lot today.
I need to exercise,
   to drink water,
   to eat.
The kitchen is a mess, so first, I need
   to clean the counters,
   to clean the dishes,
   to sweep.
I haven't yet vacuumed this week either, so I need to vacuum
   the living room.
To do that, I need to pick up the floor.
To do that, I need to pick up the dirty clothes.
To do that, I need to put away the clean laundry.
I have now raced through every room of my house, but
nothing is done yet.
Next, I might take a nap.

2022
THESE POEMS WERE WRITTEN AS I BEGAN TO
LEARN ABOUT BUDDHISM, AND AS MY WIFE AND
I ATTEMPTED TO CONCEIVE A CHILD THROUGH
FERTILITY TREATMENTS AND SPERM DONATION.

This Too
01/15/2022

I sometimes miss the taste of the last drop of alcohol I will
     ever have.
This too is impermanent.
I can feel the joints in my legs resist cycling motions.
This too is impermanent.
I feel a sense of anxiety washing over me.
This too is impermanent.
I see the faces of my parents, and smile and wave to them.
This too.
I hold my wife in my arms.
This too.
I feel my head pulse and ache.
This too.
I feel breath enter and leave my body.
This too.

Truth
01/17/2022

Once, a mathematics professor told me that logic cannot
     discern 'Truth'.
Logic can only discern validity inside the universe of facts
     that it has.
Our concept of 'Truth', in contrast, is too subjective.
Objectivity is the only realm logic can make deductions in.
Others have said 'Truth' is in the eye of the beholder.
Or that 'Truth' is concrete and written down, and only the
     'Truth' will set you free.
Human minds are small.
Our aliveness is always changing.
Of all the impermanent things, is 'Truth' the one exception?
Only time will tell.

Descriptions

10/2022

I am but a man.
Can a man be great?

I can learn.
Does that make me smart?

I can build.
Does that make me an architect?

I am productive.
Does that make me the best?

I can solve problems.
Does that make me clever?

I exist masculinely.
Does that make me a man?

Adoption Is Trauma
10/2022

I don't remember loving you.

I remember being scared.
I remember hope.
I remember loss.
I remember confusion.

I wished to be normal.
I wished to belong.
I wished to be accepted.

You didn't provide what I needed.

So I don't need you now.

I built a life I love without you.
I intend to keep it.

True Love

10/2022

Thich Nhat Hanh says I should love all beings the way that I love you.

I am not a wise man, but I don't see how that can be done.

Your love is kind, compassionate, joyous, and inclusive.

The love I feel for you is like the sweetest wine, but there is no hangover.

I don't know how I could feel this depth for every being.

My heart may well explode from the enormity of such love.

I will be a very happy and peaceful man if I can ever achieve such love.

In the meantime, I will bask in the love we have and let it wash over me in every moment that I can.

The Fallacy of Best
10/2022

We all want to do what's best.

For ourselves
For our children
For our families
For our careers
For our communities
For our nations

But 'best' is fleeting
It is unknowable
It is ever-changing

The 'best' intentions are often the path to suffering.

We cannot do what's best in every case
    because we cannot predict the future.

I propose we instead strive to answer:

What's kind?
What's helpful?
What causes the least suffering?
What feels just?
What is loving?
What can we be proud of having done here?

Life is a river, and the best that we can do is to ride the
    rapids we are on today and hope for calmer waters ahead.

One Listener, One Presence

2022

The clamor of travelers

The slamming of doors

The announcing of the intercom

The booming of jet engines

The crying of children

The yelling of mothers

The commotion

The chirping of crickets

The running of water

The singing of the birds

The patter of walking

The rustling of leaves

The stillness

These all belong
And were all observed
By one listener, with one presence

Oncoming Regret
11/2022

How can I lose you?
What will I say when I talk to you for the last time?
Will I know it's our last conversation?
What will I come to regret?
How can I know that I've done enough?
How can I say goodbye?
How can I protect myself from the grief of my siblings?
How much pain will I feel on their behalf?
How can I know if you blame me?
Would you tell me if I could ask, or would you let me believe
    I've done no wrong?
How can I ever repay you when I owe you my very life?

I guess I'll never know, but I hope I've made you proud.

To My Baby
11/2022

I hope you are never able to understand how badly I've
    wanted to meet you.
How desperate I have been to hold you, to tell you,
    "I love you" for the first time.

I long every day to know the color of your eyes, your favorite
    song, the name of your best friend.
I want so much to ask for your opinions, to hear your laugh.
I can't wait to call myself your father, to be the first man in
    your life.

One day, if I am brave, I will let you read this verse.
That is, if you don't stumble on it first.

I hope it gives you the smallest glimpse of
    what you meant to me,
    what you mean to me now,
    and what I hope I will one day mean to you.

                                     Love,
                                     Dad

Autumn Comes (I)

11/2022

The maple trees
    have been bare
    for weeks now

The towering oaks
    have only a few
    clinging leaves to shed

The grass has stopped
    its endless climb

The birds have softened
    their morning song

The sun says good night
    much earlier now

The people mow leaves
    instead of grass

The frogs have gone quiet
    and so have the crickets

The Earth is spinning
    and tilting
    as it does every year

It makes me wonder,
    "What will be different
    the next time
    the maple leaves
    are bare?"

Anxiety Was Already Here (II)

11/2022

The maple leaves
    have littered the yard
    for months now

The oak leaves
    have clogged every gutter
    on my home

The grass has browned
    and has lost its luster

The woodpeckers have torn
    holes in the siding

There are not enough hours
    of daylight
    to fix everything

The yardwork piles up
    higher than I can climb
    as it does every year

It makes me sigh,
    "What will be left undone
    when the maples
    have beaten me to spring?"

Love Saved Me

A Complicated Father

11/2022

One day, you will come into my life.

You'll be your own person,
    with your own feelings.

I promise to be honest.
To tell you the truth
    Of your conception
    Of my gender
    Of my conception
    Of my family

With that information will come feelings,
    and I promise to let you feel them.

You may be sad, or hurt.
You may not care at all.
You may pretend not to.
You may love me anyway.
You may hate me.

I will love you
    no matter what
    you think and feel.

I hope you understand why your Mom and I
    took the paths that we did.

We love you so much,
    and we always will.

You are my baby, no matter what.
I hope you learn to love me that way too.

Your Grandpa

11/2022

My dad (your Grandpa)
    isn't the smartest man.

He only got a high school education,
    but he put food on our table
    working with his hands.

My dad (your Grandpa),
    isn't the kindest man.

He loses his temper a lot,
    and no one can get on my last nerve
    the way that he can.

My dad (your Grandpa),
    isn't the most spiritual man.

But he taught me right from wrong,
    and how to leave things better
    than I found them.

He may not be perfect,
    but he is mine.

I owe him gratitude, for everything
    that I have earned in this life.

I hope he gets to meet you,
    and I hope you will remember him.

He's mine, and he'll soon be yours.

Just as I am.

Fragile Peace

12/2022

The baby is asleep
So are his Mom and Dad
So are his siblings
So is his Aunt

I watch with trepidation
Soon his Papaw will bring his Mamaw home
Soon the dog will bark
Soon his siblings will play and shout
Soon he will begin to cry

The peace is welcome,
    but it cannot last long.

I shall enjoy it while I can.

Undisputedly

12/2022

My throat throbs with pain.
My wife's is equally swollen.
My uvula gags me,
    and prevents my sleep.

I wear a mask in my own home.
I fear getting my elderly father sick.
I miss multiple days of work.
I pay for appointments and medication.

It is all worth it.

I love seeing my nieces and nephews.
I love spending time with my wife's parents and siblings.
I yearn for the time away from the house.
Even the sickness itself
    is a welcome distraction
    from my daily life.

I would do it again.

2023

THESE POEMS WERE WRITTEN DURING THE PEAK OF OUR INFERTILITY JOURNEY, AND CAPTURE OUR PIVOT TO ADOPTION.

If I Turn 81

01/2023

If I should be lucky enough to see the Earth slide around the
sun 81 times, to see 29,586 radiant risings and settings of
that wondrous star

I hope that I am happy.
I hope that my family is with me.
I hope that my cake has buttercream icing.
I hope I can dance and laugh and sing.
I hope I know that it is a Monday.

But most of all, I hope that I am kind.
I don't want to be angry, or jealous, or greedy.
I hope I am never selfish or rude.

Just Kind.

6 Years

01/23/2023

I promised to love you
    in sickness and in health
    in poverty and in wealth
    in depression and in joy
    in stress and in relaxation

I will always love you
    when your hair turns gray
    when your body decays
    when the human race has faded
    when the sun explodes
    when the universe itself is a memory

The love we share connects us
    across all of space and time.

It is boundless,
    endless,
    and everlasting.

I can't wait to love you forever.
In this life, and whatever may come next.
No matter how far apart our physical bodies may be.

To a Future Survivor
01/2023

There's no right answer when someone you love hurts you.
You want to run,
    but you feel tethered.
You want to be close to them
    and let things be as they once were.
But your heart knows they can't.
You desperately want them to change,
    but you know the ugly truth.
If they wanted to, they would have by now.

So you make excuses for their behavior.
You dance and weave around the idea of leaving.
The hurt continues.
The scars singe and overlap old scars, slowly covering every
    part of your body and mind.

You feel enclosed, and when those who truly love you
    prompt you to leave, you feel extreme pressure.
Like your very body will be torn apart by the decision.
You know what you must do for yourself and your family,
    but you don't feel like you deserve it.

I hope you find freedom.
I hope that your mental chains fall away.
I hope your life gets lighter and sunnier.
That your heart will be softened one day.
I wish that I could protect you,
    or that we could wish the scars away together.

Trust Love

01/2023

Even my worst days
    are filled with joy.

Even on rainy days
    the sun rises.

Even at funerals
    flowers bloom.

Even under extreme stress
    diamonds are formed.

Even wracked with anxiety
    confidence peeks through.

Even through illness
    Love cradles me.

Even through the reddest anger
    compassion lives within me.

Even when all is dark
    the light is waiting.

I strive to never let my fear
    overcome my faith in Love.

The Moment
01/2023

Have you ever experienced "The Moment"?

That infinitesimal feeling when everything changes.
When you finally know how something you've waited for
    will turn out.

The fleeting sensation that it all paid off
    or was all for naught.

How often is that Moment positive?
That you feel the surging pride saying,
    "I made that happen."

That positive, claimable Moment is rare and precious.
The next time you find it, be sure to cherish it.

The Woodpecker
01/2023

Rat-a-tat-tat goes the woodpecker on the timbers.
His feathers gleam in the sun, glinting as his beak
pummels his potential home.

He never stops.
You cannot scare him away for long.

In the face of loud and scary deterrents,
he simply picks up his beak,
hops a few lateral steps,
and begins anew.

I admire his persistence.

The Peace Lily

01/2023

My brother, Jeffrey, was killed in 2018.
I wasn't as close to him as I wish I had been.
But it's far too late for that now.

My mother was given a peace lily after he passed.
But the giver was the woman who had previously
    given birth to me.
And I still struggle with my relationship with her.

My mother nor I had spoken to that woman in over 3 years.
She had made it clear that I would never be
    the child she wanted.
But through tragedy, this gift still came.
A moment of kindness in spite of the pain and hatred.

We still don't really talk.
The peace lily can't change her opinion of me
    or mine of her.

My mother loves that lily; it reminds her of my brother.
It reminds me of someone I'd rather forget.

But I love my mother.
So I water the peace lily.

If We Adopt
01/2023

I was once a selfish man.
The idea of sharing my child with their birth parents scared
    me, and it made me think of my own broken relationship
    with my birth mother.

I wanted to focus on making their life amazing, and I wanted
    to shelter them from the pain I had felt.

I wanted them to have a stable family, with two parents who
    love each other. No more, and no less.

I wondered though
    Could their experience be better than mine?
    Could they find a love and connection I never found?

I used to think I dare not risk it.
I now realize that Love, no matter where it comes from,
    is not something to deny my child.

To A Beloved Friend
01/2023

A wise monk wrote,
    "the heart of spirituality
    and the mind of love
    could not be extinguished by death."

Your death is tragic.
You leave a young family,
    a single father,
    two children, your whole world,
    a church,
    and a community,
    we all grieve you so deeply.

But I still feel your spirit and your Love.
They burn bright like the summer sun.
You leave behind kindness,
    wisdom,
    and a deep compassion.

Your life is one to be celebrated.
Your voice has made the world a brighter, kinder place.

Your Love will radiate through the mountains and the ages.
I breathe with you now, and invite your loving presence.
Just as a cloud never dies, neither does the memory
    of a kind and loving being.

Thank you for helping me learn to know kindness and Love.
I hope only to be your continuation,
    showing others the kindness and Love you showed me.

To My Kerosene Heater
02/2023

You occupy space in my garage.
If we're being honest,
    that's all you've done around here for years.
Your dusty white body and flimsy metal frame are best at
    being support beams for spider webs.

I now have a robust HVAC system, which I keep routinely
    maintained.
I now keep a deep reserve of firewood to burn in our stove.
Hell, I could run the oven to produce heat, in a pinch.

But no matter how logical your removal seems, any time I try
    to pick you up and free you from my garage -

    Suddenly, I am 14 again
    Curling up in every blanket I can find
    Shoveling the gravel driveway
    Forcing my heart to pump warm blood to my extremities.
    Leaving the mountain on the third day
    Passing signs that proclaim
    "AEP DOESN'T CARE IF WE FREEZE"
    Coming back a week later, just to see if the power is back
    Checking that the pipes haven't yet shattered
    Waiting another week to be able to go home
    Hoping this time it will be warmer inside than out

I come back to my garage,
    my hands trembling on your handle.
I think I'll let you stay a little while longer, old friend.

Heaven and Hell
02/2023

Heaven is not a far away place
　　With cherubim and horns
　　With light and singing

Hell, similarly, is not a distant realm
　　With demons and ghosts
　　With fire and brimstone

　　At least, not to me.
　　Both, however, are very real.

　　Surprised?
　　You have been to both, just like I have.

　　Heaven is a mother holding her newborn son.
　　Hell is the same mother picking out a tiny casket.

　　Heaven is two lovers sharing their wedding vows.
　　Hell is the bride hearing that her groom has been
　　unfaithful.

　　Heaven is a sunny, breezy summer day.
　　Hell is a hurricane ripping homes and families apart.

　　We recognize these places without a map.
　　For Heaven and Hell are not destinations, they're
　　moments.

　　May we all bring about more trips
　　for ourselves and those around us
　　to Heaven than Hell.

Love Saved Me

Good Enough

03/2023

What does it even mean to be 'good enough'?
    At work?
    At school?
    At being a son?
    A husband?
    A father?
    A friend?

Is it something we convince ourselves of?
Or something objective?
Could it be both?
Does it even matter?

This poem does not offer an answer.
For now, simply asking is good enough.

Star Stuff
03/2023

"Are there living beings which do not call Earth their
    home?"
Humans have pondered this question since they first learned
    Earth wasn't a lonely planet, but had many space siblings.
Some might say, "Of course not, we are specially molded,
    and special to God."
Others, "Of course, we are a product of evolution, which
    likely happened more places than here."

I can't say with certainty either way.
But I know for sure that when I close my eyes and sip tea, I
    can feel the water in it, the leaves, the sun and soil that
    made the leaves, and the star stuff in the sun and the soil
    and the water.
And I know that whoever is or isn't out there among the
    stars, they too are made from the same star stuff.

So no matter what, all living beings are my kin.
They too belong and are deserving of Love.

On Authority

03/2023

"I have more money than you have."
"I have lived longer than you have."
"I have more accolades and titles than you have."
"I have read more books than you have."
"I have earned a higher title than you have."

These are all terrible reasons to let someone tell you what to
    do or think.
Instead, I choose to listen to those who say,

"I have lost more than you have."
"I have sacrificed more than you have."
"I have listened more than you have."

Above all, I respect the people who have loved with their
    whole hearts, openly and freely.

If Today Was the Last
03/2023

If you should die
    before I wake

I pray you go
    in peace

If our words today
    should be the last

I pray I said
    the best ones

If we should never
    meet again
I pray I did enough

The First Mother
03/2023

She has countless children.
She holds each one close to her every day.
She has heard all of our names.
She has seen history that we are too young to remember.
She birthed many kinds of children.

Bacteria with no eyes or ears to observe her.
Plants with roots that grab and cling to her.
Animals that dig into her for warmth.
And humans, the most selfish of all her children.

May we all learn to love our mother and our siblings
    as we love ourselves.

Vernal Equinox
03/2023

The birds have been singing for a few weeks now, ducking
    back into their nests when we have a cold snap.
They are eager to cross over from winter into spring.
The sun peeks out more often than before and occasionally
    bursts forth with radiance, defying the clouds who try to
    hold back the warmth.
This light ushers in the change.

New sprouts come up from the damp soil, clamoring to see
    the sun's light for the first time.
New buds form on the trees, waking up the great old
    creatures from their yearly rest.

I, too, am waking up, albeit more slowly
    than the ecosystem that surrounds me.
As I become more proximal to suffering, I give what I can.
I practice diligence like a strongman perfecting his grip.
I train my mind and meditate on the things I've learned.
I try to open my heart
    to widen the circle
    even though the stretching can be painful at times.
I hope one day to awaken to the insight that is within me.
Just as the Earth awakens to a new spring.

Well-Worn, Well-Loved
03/2023

The familiar button presses of a game you have loved for
    many years.
The curves of the road to your childhood home.
The feeling of the pen between your fingers as your signature
    spills onto the page.
Opening the lock on your front door.
The taste of your favorite fast food sandwich.
The drumbeat and lyrics to your favorite hype song.
The intro to your favorite sitcom.
The seat of your family sedan.
The smell of your favorite relative's home.
The taste of the candy you loved most as a child.

Some sensations wear warm, comforting patterns into the
    grooves of our brains.

Cherish these, give yourself the space to come back to them.
Let yourself enjoy these familiar sensations.
Revel in them, even if only for a moment.

A Recovering Anger Addict
04/2023

It can be hard to let go of the anger that boils inside me.
I feel it when prompted by any irritation just strong enough
    to make me grit my teeth and clench my fists.
I find that external pressures and busy world news lower this
    threshold.
That if there is already stress,
    it is much easier to make me into a swearing maniac, hell-
    bent on making the world feel my fury.

I'm not quite sure where my anger stems from most days.

Fear of inadequacy?
Fear of being 'slowed down'?
Worry about the world and the future my kids will live in?
Fear that I won't even have children?

I can't be sure on any given day.
But I am reminding myself now, and you, dear Reader,
That anger is only fear hiding behind a scary mask.
And with Love, we can gently remove the mask,
    and help it feel safe once more.

Gravity's Embrace
04/2023

The moon pulls on me tonight.
As if to tell me, "You and I are friends."
I know that much of my world can be reduced to equations
    and diagrams, to facts and figures.
But I still feel the moon's pull
    and the Earth's warm embrace.
I can feel the aliveness of space and matter.
I can confidently respond, "Yes, we are friends."
I suppose some might call me a lunatic.
But how can a felt experience be completely wrong?
And who am I to say that the moon and stars
    don't feel me too?

I Heard We Were On Stage 7
04/2023

The breath quivers as it enters my mouth and nose,
    traveling all the way into my overworked lungs.
My heart beats fast, pumping blood to the parts
    of the human body that have been honed to keep me
    safe.
My skin shivers
My muscles tense
My head pulses, hot blood coursing around my brain,
    searching for a solution to the Solution I fear.

    I know my scars mark a target on my chest,
    that my medical history is not invisible to the naked eye.

I don't know how bad it could get in my lifetime,
But I've seen the signs, the headlines,
    and the history others have lived through.
I don't think that my fears are really the same as theirs -
Those who have seen the worst of humanity firsthand,
    who have faced genocide and war.
Still I pray tonight
    For peace,
    For listening,
    For understanding,
    For Love to win, before we reach a point of no return.

I can only hope that, if I get to be a grandparent,
I will be able to tell my descendants that I was brave.
That I kept us safe,
That I loved even my most sinister enemies,
And that they, in time, came to love me back.

Blessed Are the Resilient
05/2023

May you always rise to meet the road that lies before you.
May you have the strength to face the fury of the wind.
May you prepare for the rain,
    and may it flow off your back like a duck.
Until we meet again, may you know peace.

Time Passing
05/2023

Each month that passes
My heart breaks
I miss my son, my daughter
I want to hold you
To see you grow
I hope that one day soon
I will get to meet you

Ode to the Queen of Mars

06/2023

Oh, to be royalty!

To be praised and worshiped by strangers.

I will never feel the rush of being the King of anything.

But listening to the *Queen of Mars*
    puts a smile on this peasant's face.

May we all find moments that make us feel
    the way that Candace did on Mars.

On a New Path

07/2023

When you are older,
  you will ask
  about your origin

I promise to be honest with you
  and to tell you anything
  you may wish to know

Your origin may be messy
  and it may be a long time
  before you get to meet your Mom and me

But I am holding fast to the prospect
  of holding you in my arms
  and raising you to be a great person

One day, I hope to watch your success.
To cheer from the sidelines as you achieve your dreams
I already love you so much.

Worth It

07/2023

Changing the path to you was terrifying.

Will you resent me?
Will you yearn for a kind of family I cannot provide?
Will you one day pierce me with the sharpest sword,
    "You're not my real Dad"?

How long will we wait for you?
How many times will we come close to finding you,
    but fall short?

I stand at the beginning of this path
    with a mixture of hope and fear in my chest.

I hope one day that I can explain to you these feelings.
I look forward to learning how you feel about it.
We will one day swap notes.
I truly hope that your experience surpasses mine.

I hope also that you have as much love for me as I do for
    you and for my own parents.
I know already that I love you more than life itself.

I cannot wait to meet you.
But wait I must, and wait I shall.
Because it will have been worth it.

The Home Study
10/2023

The social worker came this week.
The one who will decide if I am worthy of my dreams.
    Measuring,
    noting,
    interrogating every detail of our life and home.

She seemed satisfied with our environment.
But I still worry.

How can it be that so much of my future
    is in the hands of a woman I've met once?
I pray she decides that we are safe and loving.
And even then, if we be marked by her seal of approval,
    that will have been but the first hurdle.

I have so much love to give to my children.
But for now, only an empty nursery to pour it into.

Trained On Trauma

10/2023

I am still learning.
I do not have all the answers.
You will enter my life with a history
    that I may never truly know.
I can't protect you from that.

But I will love you.
I will do my best to smother the pain with warm hugs.
I will wipe your tears and let you know how happy I am that
    you were born,
    and that you are my child.
Even now,
    before you have even been conceived,
    I know that your life will be hard
But I will do my very best to make it easier for you.

Moments That Shine

10/2023

How can I be so good, and feel so bad?

Why do my achievements often feel so hollow,
    and so far in the past or the future?

Victories crystallize for a fleeting moment
    and shatter into memories

May I teach my children to let that crystal gem
    sparkle and shine
    and keep pieces of it in their sock drawer.
So that they might pull it out and let it catch the light
    on a dark day.

Just Like Me

10/2023

You won't have my eyes.
But may you have a light that burns in them through the
    darkest trials.
Just like mine.

You won't have my smile.
But may you strive to make those around you smile.
Just like me.

You won't have my quads.
But may you love a sport the way that I love cycling.

I hope you never have
    my anxiety,
    or my depression
    or my GI issues.

But if you do,
    I am confident
    that I will bestow upon you
    the strength
    to face life's challenges.
Just like me.

Nobody's Got That Range

10/2023

Who could know that I would be here today?

Living in the suburbs of Columbus

Loving plants as much as sports

Loving a beautiful woman and her incredibly loud dog

Praying a baby will enter my life

Making dinner for my wife and my parents

Buying Christmas gifts for my in-laws

Loving every moment, unexpected as it may be

Consistency

12/2023

The sand drips through the hourglass at the same rate
    all the time.

Even when you are waiting for your life to change.

Time has no opinion
    no agenda
    it continues ticking away
    blissfully unaware.

Whether you wait for a call
    or a letter
    or a decision
    or a birth
    or a death

Time moves the same at every bell and buzzer
And at all the moments in between.

2024

My Nebulous Father
02/2024

There's something wonderful about not knowing the identity
    of my biological father.

Sure, my doctors ask uncomfortable questions, and my
    parents had to have some awkward conversations
    when I was a kid.

But my father - he could be anyone I meet.

When I listen to old labor songs,
    he's a broad, bearded Scotsman,
    breaking his back in the mines.

When I listen to sea shanties,
    he's a tall marine, spending his days at sea,
    the spray of the ocean stinging his face.

When I tan and take in the summer sun,
    he's an Arab man whose ancestors ruled the desert,
    much like the Dad I grew up with.

When I watch football,
    he's an ex-linebacker,
    drinking and laughing right beside me.

When I eat authentic Mexican food,
    he's an immigrant laborer,
    and maybe I have his mustache.

I can connect to any man,
    from any class or creed,
    because he could be my own father.

There Are Only Two Favorite Colors

02/2024

What's your favorite color?

How do you know that?
Are you sure?

Let me stop you, let's take a step back.
Maybe it's a phase, most people like you don't like that color.

Can't you just try harder to like this other color better?

What do you mean your favorite color changed? Then the
other one must never have really been your favorite.

Well, you can say it's your favorite, but I still think you like
the other one better.

You'll change your mind later.

You're just confused.

You're not exactly like the other people who like that color,
you know.

Don't you dare tell kids you like that color,
it might confuse them.

You're a liar.
It's just a fantasy.
People like you make me sick.

No matter what you do, I will never respect
Your favorite color.

Freedom

02/2024

Pulse: 81
Blood Pressure: 103/77
Blood Glucose: 82
O2: 96%

These may look to you, dear reader, like a misprint.

Like I've confused my poetry book with my medical log.

But for me, these numbers are the resounding chime of the
    Liberty Bell.
The last piece of tape on a particularly stubborn package.

These numbers show me that I **can** be healthy,
    and I can manage my stress successfully.

The chains of bad habits formed over decades
    are beginning to bend.

My intention is beginning to be fulfilled.

Reader, I beg you -
    take care of your body.
There is no freedom like
    a healthy vessel
    to carry you through the storms of life.

Totality
04/08/2024

New things make me anxious
Traffic can be terrifying
Talking to strangers?
    Oh, no, thank you
Finding city parking
Taking the Grand Tour of a brand new office building
Holing up, trying to drown out the noise
    of other people working.

Awkward "Where are you?" chatter ensues on all my calls.
Checking the time repeatedly
Until it is finally time to nervously step outside,
    put on my flimsy glasses,
    and look up, hoping to see a wonder.

My God, it was worth it.
Just me and half a dozen strangers
Dancing, singing, and marveling at the wonders of life
All life stood still to watch in awe with us
    the birds stopped singing, the cars stopped rolling
It was a truly interconnected experience
The Earth, Moon and stars didn't stand still,
    but everyone under the moon did
We stood in great wonder
Sharing this unique experience together
In total darkness
And total peace.

Noon Prayer

04/2024

The sun peeks through the clouds today.
It has rained much of the day, and it will certainly rain more.
The Tiktok weathermen insist I'm in danger
    in spite of this calm.
I know good and well that the calm cannot stay,
    but I know the same will be true of the storm.

If the rolling clouds and raging winds should come to take
    me or my family tonight,
    May they know how much I loved them.
    May they know peace.
    May none of us suffer.
    May we have the strength to go on no matter what.

Wisdom of Ages

04/2024

I wonder for what reason
    I have lived 28 years
    and am only just now realizing
    the great wisdom
    which humanity achieved
    thousands of years ago.

Stoics, Buddhists, Christians,
    all the wise men and women
    have written the same truth:
    the key to peace
    is a peaceful mind.

How did my ancestors miss this?
How did they cling to a God who judges
    over a Father who whispers calm and ease?
Why did they stumble through darkness
    while the secret was within them all along?
Perhaps some did know,
    and simply neglected to pass it on,
    their wisdom lost to the ages
    before it could reach me.
Perhaps the message did reach me,
    and I was simply deaf to it
    clinging to my own ignorance.

For whatever reason, I never knew:
    emotional regulation sharpens the mind.
And if you control your mind,
    you control your life.

I intend to ensure my children know
    the value of a smile, a deep breath, and a simple prayer.

Increasing Difficulty
07/2024

It's hard now, and I fear it will be harder for you than it was
    for your mother and me.

I don't mean to scare you, but I do mean to prepare you.

I wish my generation and those who came before me
    had made it easier for you,
    but I know that we are not doing enough.
    I see plastic swirling in the ocean,
    hurricanes growing stronger each year.
    Violent extremists set the world on fire,
    and children don't feel safe at school.

I'll help you as much as I can in my lifetime,
    but in the end,
    the burden will pass to you when I am gone.
    You'll fight battles we never dreamed of,
    flooded cities and scorched earth,
    fighting for truth in a world drowning in lies.
    You'll have to face hatred that hides in the shadows
    and violence that breaks into the light.
I wish I could shield you from all of it.

May I lighten your load as much as I can

May your world be safer, healthier, and happier than mine.

Jesus Loves Me Too
08/2024

I still sing *Jesus Loves Me*
I never mean to, but sometimes when I am alone
    the familiar tune comes to me,
    unbidden, but not unwelcome.

I don't always know if I believe the literal words anymore.
But the melody always soothes me.
It helps me to remember that **someone** loves me
Whether Jesus does or not,
    I leave to your interpretation
    I choose to believe He does.
Either way though,
    my wife,
    my parents,
    my sister,
    my friends,
    I know they love me.
The Bible doesn't have to tell me so,
    their actions say it all.
Their promise is real,
    and I see them stand up for me.
I don't always see Christians do that.

Maybe I'll sing it a little differently for my kids:
    Daddy loves me
    This I know
    For he always tells me so
    He protects me, big and strong,
    He'll be with me my whole life long.

That way, no matter what they believe,
    they never forget how much I love them.

Jesus *IS* Love
08/2024

I don't know why it took me so long to understand this
core teaching.
I glossed right over it, believing instead that Jesus was an
evangelical, and that He hated me.
As I learned more about Love and compassion,
it finally hit me.

This is the crux of the American experiment.
We. Believe. In. The. Good.

We believe in the most high,
the strongest Force
and we believe that it is Good.

We believe that we can do all things because we have the
Good on our side.
We know that we will be safe, and that allows us to take
risks, and to innovate.
We know that Love can bind up wounds and heal our
communities of the deepest divides.

The Bible shows us God's character arc:
He gives up the violence of the Old Testament.
He sends a savior.
Jesus preaches to love one another.
To build up the broken.
To be the hands of God protecting our neighbors.

Why would we ignore
the most important message that God ever sent?

He represents Love itself.
How could anyone hate or kill in His name?
How could you share this Love with others today?

The Bible Has Context
09/2024

Why do we pick individual verses out of the Bible?
Why do we teach our children to memorize it,
    as if it is a badge of honor
    to repeat particular phrases
    with no knowledge of what they may mean?

There is no other text that I've seen people treat
    as if it is a menu, picking off the numbers they like.

    Some may take,
    "An eye for an eye" (Exodus 21:24),
    as a call for vengeance.
    Yet, later we read:
    "Turn the other cheek" (Matthew 5:39),
    a call for forgiveness.

    How can we separate these teachings
    from their time, their context, their authors?

Should it not be read as a collection of books?
    Each with an author
    Each with a history
    Each with a perspective
    Each with a context
    Each with a voice

The Bible is no more univocal
    than the people it was written for.

    Each verse tied to its time and place,
    just as we are.

Love Saved Me
09/2024

She loved me for who I really was.

Not for my coverings
    nor my body
    nor my faults
    nor my status
    nor my salary.

She loved **me.**

Before I even knew how to love myself.
When I was ready to destroy this body, hating it so deeply,
She saw through to my essence, my truest self.
And we, there, were good.
We understood each other.
I saw her exactly the same,
    and I loved her right back.

    I realized then, just as I do now,
    that all my closest relationships have this same quality.
    My family,
    my best friend,
    my wife,
    my teachers,
    my church,
    my coworkers -
    They all saw past who I was pretending to be,
    straight to my spirit.

I resolve to do that for others now.
To see their best even when they can't see it.

Rootless

09/2024

I too have no roots.
Mine were severed far less brutally than others,
    and certain pain can know no match.
But our hurts are kin.
We are connected by this loss.
I grieve deeply that my own ancestors
    were the cause of such anguish and separation.
In the spirit of understanding,
    let me tell you where my roots are severed:

My mother did not know my father's name,
    and I shall never learn it.

My mother's father did not know his father either,
    nor did he know the fathers and mothers before them.
For they were in a far off land, oceans away.

My mother then left me to seek solace in substances,
    and upon her return,
    she denounced me and my new parents.
The same family who raised me
    and taught me to Love all colors and creeds.

My mother's mother also wrote to inform me
    that I would be damned.
I never got to hear her speak again.
I hate cancer.

My Dad cut away ties with my new siblings
    and my Mom's kin
His temper and intolerance of them and their ideas
    drove a wedge.
I suspect that the wedge would lie the same
    for my sins

Either way, I could form no ties.

But for my church and family who loved me radically
    I may have been a dangerous and violent teen.
But these bonds kept me here among the living
    and because they have Loved me
    I know for certain that some good force
    is behind the curtain

So I Lift My Voice and Sing
For the Union that can tear down hatred
We plant our roots here, in America
Interweaving our stories with those who came before us
    and breaking the chains of all the downtrodden
For this Land hosts any brave ones
    and sets them free.

Habit Substitution
09/2024

When I get the urge to snack,
    I try to instead crochet a row
    in a beautiful, hand crafted gift
    of a heart
    or a chicken
    or some other cute trinket.

When it is finished,
    I gift it to a neighbor
    anonymously leaving
    a small token of joy
    on their doorstep.

A Prayer for Labor
09/09/2024

Tonight, I sit on my cushion in contemplation,
    incense burning,
    silence my only companion.

As I sit, I smile as new life crosses my mind.

A new baby is to arrive in the coming days.

Her mother will bring forth a new niece,
    screaming, full of life not yet lived.

May mother and daughter be happy,
    may they be healthy,
    may they be safe,
    may the expansion of our family be joyous.

The Witness
09/2024

Today, I dedicate my life's passion
    to make this world into the place I want to live.
I will be the one who sees the mistakes I have made
    and makes the change that I want to see

I will share my voice,
    my Love,
    my time,
    my treasure,
    and my talents
    for the cause of soothing suffering
    and bringing people together in Love.

We can create Heaven on Earth together,
    and I am here to witness it.

Learning By Loving
09/2024

Museums are essential;
    they are the very lifeblood of a culture.

For in a museum, one must confront
    their past,
    the past of their oppressors,
    and the past of their victims.
One must learn to forgive and be forgiven
    when confronted with the reality of our shared history.

One cannot deny a tragedy
    which they have seen firsthand,
    and for which they have shed real tears.

Language
09/2024

I have come to the painful realization
that certain words would be better off unwritten.

I am pained by the knowledge that I live in a world
where suffering is so common,
where people are so cruel,
that we needed to come up with the words,
"rape",
"torture",
"slavery",
"genocide"

My calling is to make these atrocities so rare
that we forget what we used to call them.
Let us instead be so vast in our Love,
that we learn from the Greeks
to come up with many ways
to describe Love and kindness.

Redneck Stoicism
09/2024

It's gonna be the way it's gonna be
    until it ain't.

And either way
    it's gonna be okay.

Look Up
09/2024

We argue over words, but miss the quiet light,
    rising over both of us
    beckoning, without a sound
    for us to notice it.

I point up, my hand tracing the light
    that softens the darkness.
"Look," I say without speaking,
    "there's more than this."
You glance up,
    and for just a moment
    I can see the reflection in your eyes.
You see it, too
    even if you don't fully understand it yet.

The moon sees you, too,
    and it lingers,
    a flickering thought that you carry with you.

You hold your beliefs and I mine,
    each a reflection of something deeper
    something so real
    that we both can feel it
    without saying a word.

Why can't we both exist under the same sky?
Isn't there room for both of us?
For all of us?

We are all looking to see and understand the light.
I can see it, and you can, too.

Just look up.

The Last Moment
09/2024

When the end comes, we all fall still,
　　for one breath, at least.
At that moment, we are perfectly peaceful.
We can cause no harm,
　　and we simply exist.
In that final flash,
　　I will cause no suffering
　　and that is enough.

I'm not scared.
I've put in the work,
　　and my brain has got something beautiful saved.
A Grand Finale,
　　the last fireworks of a life well-lived.
　　Bright bursts of memory and light,
　　colors of a journey complete.

I will watch it all unfold
　　like a father at a school play
　　proud and cheering
　　as my brain performs
　　his final act.
After everything we've been through together
This body and mind have worked so hard.
And it will culminate in this performance
　　a hand-crafted show.
I will watch with Love as he sends me off,
　　giving me the best he has to offer
　　a spectacular farewell.

For one moment, at least,
　　we all touch the divine,
　　not in fire or glory,
　　but in quiet understanding.

There is no fear, no hate,
    just the stillness of clarity.
There is nothing left to fight
    no more to do
    nothing to cling to.
In that stillness,
    we are parents once more
    watching the children we once were,
    watching the lives we have lived
    with Love and awe.

Peace isn't a goal to be chased.
It has been within us all along
    just waiting for the perfect moment to be revealed.

Memory

09/2024

I don't want a statue
    or stories in history books.

But I do hope that,
    years from now,
    someone might say,
    "I remember
    how my papaw
    left small gifts,
    little hearts,
    crocheted with love
    on our neighbors' doorsteps,
    and how it made him smile
    even if he never saw them receive it."

That would be enough.

The Seeds We Water

09/2024

We all walk the same road -
   Siddharta beneath the Bodhi tree,
   Jesus healing the sick,
   Mahatma Gandhi spinning threads of justice,
   Clara Barton mending wounds on the battlefield,
   Martin Luther King Jr marching with hope in his heart,
Each of them, like us,
   born to this soil
   each with the same seeds of Good
   waiting to be watered.

The greatest among us are not those without flaws
   but those who choose to tend their garden.
To nurture the tender shoots
   with patience, compassion, and Love
Who pour water over the seeds of others,
   lifting them up,
   helping them bloom.

Peter, once quick with the sword,
   learned to lay it down for peace.
Buddha found stillness,
   and let his mind grow.
Jesus carried forgiveness
   in every step.
Gandhi's quiet resolve
   wove the freedom of a nation.
Clara held lives in her hands
   and healed with every stitch.
Teresa cradled the poor,
   her hands full of grace.
Martin planted dreams in the hearts of millions
   his voice still waters hope.

The soil is here for us all
    rich with potential.
What matters is which seeds we water
The best among us aren't those
    without any fear or doubt.
They are those who choose
    to nurture the Good.
And who help others
    find the sunlight,
    the rain,
    and the Love
    that they need in order to grow.

We are all walking this road
    and we all carry seeds of
    Patience, Love, Kindness, Joy, Peace, and Self-control.
But we must water these seeds,
    if we are to bear fruit.

The greatest beings have produced this fruit
    and with gentle hands
    helped others to bloom too.

The Empty Nursery
09/2024

I stay busy
    I'm not avoiding it
    but I've got work to do
    things to build -
    cribs, muscles, wisdom.
That empty room,
    the cavernous space
    waits to be filled with new sounds,
    and smells,
    and Love.
It's not just a reminder of what's missing -
    It reminds me of what's coming.

I've seen people wait and struggle for years
    I stand with them now
    Loving and hurting
    and hoping the whole way
I go to those hurt places
    with helping hands,
    where all is quiet,
    and all we have left
    is the hope
    that Joy is on its way.

It's not about keeping the silence away
It's about filling it
    with Love and Hope
    and all the best Fruits
So that my child might taste them
    sooner than I did.

THE ELECTION OF 2024
THESE POEMS WERE WRITTEN WHILE I WAS ON
THE CAMPAIGN TRAIL, INSPIRED BY LEADERS
WHOSE HOPE, RESILIENCE, AND OPTIMISM FOR
THE FUTURE REIGNITED MY OWN. THEIR VISION
AND DETERMINATION GAVE ME THE STRENGTH
TO FIGHT FOR THE VALUES I HOLD DEAR IN
WAYS I HADN'T BEFORE. THIS CHAPTER
REPRESENTS THE PEAK OF MY PERSONAL
JOURNEY, REFLECTING THE JOY AND PURPOSE
I'VE FOUND ALONG THE WAY. IT IS THIS VERY
HOPE THAT MOTIVATES ME TO SHARE THESE
WORDS WITH THE WORLD.

The Death of Hope
08/2024

I remember the moment that my hope died.
I was in college, it was January 10th, 2017.
I sat with bated breath watching
President Obama's farewell address.

He tried to give me hope, faith, and courage.
But I, like the crowd, didn't know how to let him go.

I didn't listen.
I disengaged.
I was isolated.

He tried to tell us that Americans are fighters,
and that I would be entrusted with the fight.
But instead of listening to the man I admired so much, I
decided to learn that the hard way that freedom isn't free.

In the coming years, I became terrified.
My brother was killed, there was fighting in the streets,
and there stood I, clinging tightly to my weapons, putting
my physical safety above all else.

But suddenly, two new players entered the field,
singing those old tunes of hope and resilience,
reminding me of the America I once loved so dearly.

Today, I feel a renewed belief
in the America that President Obama talked about.
I recognize now that letting them silence me was the
same as surrender.
Now, I'll protect that America with all my might.

May I serve as a bulwark for the America that I love
and may God open the eyes of those who still can't see it.

The Side I'm On
08/2024

I'm a tech worker, but I have been blind to the implications
    of the latter for too long.

I once aspired to become the boss, like my Dad.
I now realize that my aversion to people management is not
    a deficit, but instead, a badge of honor.

For the time being, I'm proud to be a worker.
I'm proud to contribute,
    and to build up the workers around me.

    The long hours,
    the constant uncertainty,
    the looming threat of layoffs
    They remind me that even in tech, we're not immune.
Every job I ever quit was because of a bad boss.
My best bosses, in contrast, didn't act like bosses at all.
They remembered that they are workers too.

So today, I resolve to remember Blair Mountain
    To remember the rednecks
    to honor the sit-down strikes in Flint,
    the marches in Memphis,
    the walkouts in Seattle.

To never forget my roots
    and to fight for the working man at every turn.

Power
08/2024

I worry a lot about fascism these days.

I see them saying,
    "We must eradicate them."
    "They are vermin."
    "Put they/them in the woodchipper."

I'm not sure why I didn't see it sooner, or why I participated
    in spaces where this kind of talk was going on.
Perhaps every man in his twenties finds these places.
    These dark corners where guns are worshiped.
    These echo chambers where every stranger is hell bent on
    harming you and your family.
And they convince him, "Only we can protect you."

I am ashamed of some of the affiliations
    that I made in my most extreme phase.
But I also see that this growth was important, so that I could
    understand my brothers who are still in that place.

I see now that grief can drive a man down a
    dark and lonely path littered with bodies and fear.
I see now that I can make myself and my family safe without
    cutting off the whole world around us.

May I do my part now to help the men who are still alone in
    those spaces, clinging to a community that won't protect
    them or stand up for their needs.

May I show them what Love looks like,
    and may they learn that violence can't destroy hatred
    only Love has that power.

Our Shot

08/2024

We have a chance this year to prove to the world once again
   that the American way crushes tyranny.

We have done it before:
   At Yorktown
   At Appomattox
   At Blair Mountain
   At Normandy
   At Birmingham
   At Stonewall
   At Ground Zero

We all fight the same fight,
   and our people sing the same song.
We must stand together and beat the would-be autocrats.
Not with violence, but through the power of Love.

As we have done so many times before, so we shall do now.
We look to the wisdom of the
   freedom fighters who came before us.
Who told us about peace and how community is the cure.

We do no harm, but we don't accept being harmed either.
We are the majority, for we are many cultures united.
Now let's go show them what we can do with opportunity.

Present Regret

09/2024

I wish I had done more in 2020.
I thank the protestors who fought for my brother
    when I was too scared to do it myself.
I was too scared of disease and violence to leave my home,
    and for that I carry a great shame.

On another hand,
    I also wish the conversation
    had captured the complexity of the issue.

Black lives matter.
Cops are people.
Cops murdered my brother.
All of these things can be true at once.

We can call for a change without calling for violence.
We must show them that we are peaceful
    or they will paint us as the enemy.
They see even one violent flashpoint,
    and they turn their backs to us.
They'll say we tore down their cities
    and use it to ignore the slaughter
    or worse - to justify it.

I can't help but wonder:
If I had lent my voice then,
    would more like me have understood?
I can't time travel, but I can do better now.
So I shall.

Human Resolve
09/2024

I've been crying in the shower a lot lately.

Not because I am weak, but because I care so damn much.

    About teachers fearing for their jobs and lives.
    About children learning to hate themselves at church.
    About trans women in the South terrified to go outside.
    About veterans battling wars in their own minds.
    About women dying when they should be giving life.
    About Ukrainians desperate to return home.
About Palestinians and Israelis waiting for the next bombing.

My tears do not make me weak.
They give me the strength to go on.
They are my release valve,
    letting me feel the pain,
    hear those who need help,
    and pick up the work that needs doing.

It's not time to cry - it's time to act.

Changing Communities
09/2024

Your brown neighbors aren't a threat to you.
They aren't taking your jobs.
They aren't stealing your pets.
They're living their lives,
    maybe a little differently than you do.
They're working, raising kids, going to church,
    just like you do.
Those aren't the neighbors I fear.

I fear that white neighbor - the one with the flags.
He might just hate me,
    he might threaten violence,
    he might vote my rights back a century.
His son may take up arms against me and my children
    with a weapon they bonded over.

    We are called to extend grace and love
    to everyone we meet -
    not just the neighbors we love,
    not just the neighbors we agree with.
    To every person we cross paths with,
    even the ones who frighten us.
Because it's hard to be cruel to someone
    showing you love and compassion.
For when we show them that we love them,
    they see the Fruit of the Spirit ripen in us,
    and they are left speechless.
Love is our most powerful weapon
    for it completely disarms the other side.

For The Record

09/2024

My first AR-15
    was a gift
    from a man
    who insisted
    I could not sufficiently
    protect his daughter
    without it.

He thought I lacked the strength
    to be her protector.

My acceptance
    of the weapon
    allowed us to form
    an unspoken pact
    a shared mission:
    Protect Her

    He, his daughter, and I
    have all bonded
    over our shared love
    of shooting.

    I wonder now though,
    was the weapon itself
    ever the answer?

    Did it make our family safer,
    or simply satisfy his doubts?

I am certain
    that she and I will always protect one another
    with or without
    the AR-15

Give and Take

09/2024

If responsible gun owners cannot come to the table,
    the children who survive
    the horrors we have allowed in their schools
    will not forget our failure
    and they will come for all the damn guns.

We must be willing to sit at the table
    to make compromises
    or we risk that our children
    will one day overrule us
    for their trauma will be louder than we are.

Children never forget that kind of trauma
    losing friends and teachers
    to gunfire in a place
    that should have been safe.

They are growing up already,
    standing together
    begging for a solution,
    and I choose to stand with them
    before they decide that my input
    does more harm than good.

Unity
09/2024

I want my culture back.
When I was a kid,
    it was so easy
    for everyone in my community
    to come together
    and put aside divides
    to help one another.

Elections have always made it harder
    but we were able to share football, baseball, the
    Olympics,
    blood drives, disaster relief, canned food drives,
    and any project that brought us together
    no matter our backgrounds.
I can remember the great leaders
    crossing party lines
    clearing a middle way
    for helping those in need
    putting country over party
    putting Love over hate
    putting unity over division.

I want that back!
I want to be on old Rocky Top
    and not be afraid
    to use Neyland's restrooms.
I want to see my friends living freely
    without fear.
I want to see everyone in the community
    lifting each other up, helping without hesitation.
We stand now with a choice,
    we could continue to break apart,
    or we can come together.
The choice is yours, dear reader.

Lorena
09/2024

My Spanish teacher once told me
that the only groups
that were still socially acceptable
to publicly discriminate against
were Hispanics
and LGBTQ+ folks

We laughed, but we could see the pain
in one another's eyes.

We knew it to be true, and that was hard to swallow.

As I hear MAGA crowds shouting, "SEND THEM
BACK"
I can't help but wonder - has she figured out what I have
yet?
That 'Lorena' was never safe
from a world that feared difference,
and I could never be
the person I was expected to be.
I would have to undergo metamorphosis,
to shed that name, that mask,
before I could grow my wings to fly.

Don't Just Pray, Help
09/2024

God's not your senator,
and calling him every morning can only do so much.
To have a tangible impact, God needs hands.

That is why we are called to be His hands and feet.
I have blistered mine all summer
to feed the poor
to heal the sick
to build up the lowly
to mend the broken
to bring blood to the injured
to bring hope to the weary.

We must be the agents of change in this world
and go forth to make a difference.
We are called to give our time and talents
for the good of every one of our neighbors.
For if those who seek to be like Christ won't answer His
call,
who will?

The Boys in the Holler

09/2024

The boys in the holler love Jesus and their mamas
    just like I do.

It took me longer than I care to admit
    to realize that we are very alike.

So they must know what I know, that beneath these
    mountains lies a foul, smoking evil, burning with hatred.
If these mountains could talk,
    they'd tell you horrible stories of what has been done
    to anyone too… 'different'.

I can't stay in my homeland.
I'm too sensitive to the stench
    of whispers and shameful glares
    of beatings and whippings
    of rape and death.

We know who they are
    under their hoods
    and their badges
    and their hats.

But we are the Union whose sole existence
    is to put that hate away
    in the deepest holler
    under the tightest lock.

The evil in these hills was created by our own.
We're sorry that we let it out.
We ought to know better.
One day my brothers in the holler will see it too,
    and hang their heads in shame.
But today, we march on.

Nuance

09/2024

My Dad, for all his faults, is a good man.
I know it to be true because he taught me most of my values.
    to Love my neighbor
    to leave things better than I found them.

He didn't, however, serve as a perfect role model.
He lied and cheated,
    he hated Appalachian culture,
    and he despised my Mom's family.

He gave up on them without trying to understand them.

To be clear, they weren't perfect either.
Some in my family have shot pets
    for standing in the wrong place at the wrong time.
Some more hate immigrants
    more than anything else in this world.

But the men in Appalachia were good men too.
They loved their families fiercely,
    and would die to protect them.
    I learned about security and self-reliance from them,
    how to shoot a gun,
    how to drive stick,
    how to can soup.

    I choose not to give up on them.
    I dream that one day,
    we'll live as my Dad's brother did -
    free, peaceful, and stable,
    with enough Love to go around
    and a passion for doing what's right.

I Side With Love
09/2024

I often meet people
    who simply don't understand me.
They see me reach out a helping hand and ask,
    "Why?" or, "What's in it for you?"
It's simple, really.
    Because I Love everybody.
Not just the people who "deserve" it
    but everyone,
    because everyone deserves Love
    and every damn person
    deserves to be seen.

I could let myself become jaded, like so many do.
But I choose Love
    every time
    not because it's easy
    but because it's the hardest thing to do
    to Love even your 'enemies', as Jesus did.

    Make no mistake - I'm not perfect
    I still have my moments of anger and hatred,
    but I try every day,
    to bind up my wounds,
    and the wounds of others
    so that Love may flow freely.

Once you see the divine in everyone
    it changes everything
    it all becomes worth it,
    and so much easier.

So why do I give a damn?
Because Love gives a damn,
    and there's no other side that I want to be on.

Light Through the Cracks
09/2024

When many calamities came at once,
    Christian voices called out to me
    urging me to stock up
    on ammo, food, water, and toilet paper
To fortify my heart against the world.
They cloaked themselves in righteousness to cover their fear.
They promised safety through separation.
Even then, I could see the Light through the cracks.

When the world changed,
    I clung to the promise of protection.
I was haunted by the violence that claimed my brother.
Each memory was a reminder
    of the felt safety that I had lost.
The fear nearly consumed me,
    it made arms feel like a lever of control
    but they offered no true refuge.

As the pandemic spread,
    and protests raged in the streets,
    my friends and relatives reveled in their righteousness.
Their insistence on extreme preparedness
    allowed them to believe
    that all their enemies were external
    that they could all be locked out.
But I was wrestling a battle within
    wondering whether fear
    could really protect me
    and if high walls invited peace or pain.

I saw the border
    as the stories were woven
    of migrants fleeing violence,
    seeking hope.

Love Saved Me

Only to be met with suspicion and scorn
    labeled as criminals
    for the crime of survival.
    I saw in them my own pain,
    a reminder that fear spawns demons
    and perpetuates the cycle of bloodshed and tears.

In the stillness of my mind
    I sought wisdom and peace.
I found solace in the teachings of the Buddha
    that Love is stronger than fear.
I remembered Jesus's call to Love my neighbor
    to embrace my enemies.
And I realized clearly
    the real threat is the division we create
    when we forget our sameness.

For beneath the shouts and chaos
    I could see the hurt
    and it looked just like mine.
We share a struggle
    and the cure is understanding.
Not division, and not walls.
Compassion is the balm
    that allows us to heal,
    extend Love,
    and form connections.
To defend our common Light
    against the Darkest night.

    When fear grips us,
    we must reach out
    to see the humanity in each face,
    for firearms may be the sword,
    but Love is the mightiest shield.
We must bind together
    and rise in the Light
Leaving Darkness behind forever.

Storm's Approach

09/2024

When the sky darkens and the winds rise
There's no time for packing
    no chance to flee
For those who live in the hollers
    the streets become rivers
    hope slips away
    washed out by the tide
    of neglect and indifference.

Fuel is a luxury, and the buses have long stopped.
Sirens wail as lost souls,
    left behind,
    cling desperately to their homes and families.
As their dreams are swept away
    by the furious wind and water.

The warnings reach their ears
    but it's already too late.
They don't have the means by which to flee
And most - nowhere to go
As the storm barrels toward them
    they cling to their loved ones,
    the last lifeboat.

It's easy to shame them
    to call them fools.
But we must consider -
    Where have we failed
    that our neighbors can't trust
    that we can help them?
That they would sooner perish
    than risk taking a helping hand?

Gridlock

09/2024

We all live on the edge of roads
    that lead to nowhere.
Where the road work is never done
Where the bridges are never built.
But bottles and pipes
    pass through many hands
Some chasing the pain
    with whatever they can
But aching all the same.

The old strip job is still there
    but it ain't been worked in years.
And the men who did have all been smothered
    by the black sickness in their lungs
    or have broken their backs
    from a career of work done well and done hard.
But no savings, and no pension
    await them when they're finished.

The fields stretch wide
    but the land is barren.
It won't let man grow
    it too feels the ratcheting of tension and hatred
The farmer hungers for something he can't eat
    a life he always wanted,
    just out of reach.

I once heard a woman cry for a child
    she couldn't keep
They told her she'd have to choose
    her life or her child's.
But only if the state approves
She holds the path she could not take
    like a prayer unanswered.

I've seen also my brothers
    frantic about the swords they carry.
Wondering if that felt sense of security
    will be wrested from them
They can't fathom that something like safety
    would ever be outside their control.

I sit in a pew where Love feels conditional
A salvation reserved for everyone
    - but not for me
    or my friends
The door to Heaven was locked tight
    keeping me out.
No matter how hard I knocked.

And there's a man at the border
    papers in hand,
    but he's missing something minor
He has done no wrong,
    he wants to call us neighbor
But he cannot go back for documents
    it would cost him or his children
    their very lives
So he begs, but that door is locked.

We're all stuck in the gridlock
Told to wait,
    baited and switched
Moving the goalposts
So we're somehow always wrong.
But all any of us want
    is a fair shake
    to be seen
    to be made whole
To see that the road is clear before us.

The Boy in the War Zone

09/2024

His mother whispered through the cracks in the walls.
Telling him to stay low, quiet.
His father was already gone
    taken by the men in the black boots
Stomping through their home
    louder than the thunder of artillery fire
    that only ever stopped to reload.
He didn't know how his parents became a target
To him, it didn't matter.

Now, the house is empty and cold
The Love that once lived here is but a faded memory.
The air feels too thin to breathe.
He wraps himself in his father's coat;
    it is still warm.
The soldiers have passed,
    marching on to the next home
    to shatter it, like this one.
He's not sure that they ever saw him.
To them, he's the same as the rubble.

He wants to call for his mother
    but the silence has no answer.

A Child on The Other Side

09/2024

Her father went to fight bad guys in a far away land.
Her mother says it's very important
But all she can think about
    is the empty chair
    at the head of the dining room table
    each morning, noon, and night.
Her mother works hard, morning to night
    her hands worn,
    her smile faded.

She hears the walls creak,
    and clings tightly to her favorite stuffed animal
    (the one Dad gave her).
She needs a hug,
    but Mom is still at work.
When she tells her mother that night that she was scared
    her mother sighs,
    "We all get scared sometimes, sweetheart."
She cries, "What if Dad is scared?"
    and silently fears,
    "What if he forgot about me?"

She dreams that night that Dad is home
    giving her a big hug
But when she wakes,
    it's just her and the walls again.
Mom already left for work,
    and she forgot to say goodbye

The World That Could Be

09/2024

In another world, two children sit together
    under the same sky.
But it has softened
    there is no smoke,
    no gunfire,
    no fear
Peace is carried on the breeze
    with the singing of birds
    and the laughter of children.

The boy no longer hides,
    he runs freely, lightly
    smiling from ear to ear.
Beside him is a girl, who laughs
    as she runs into her father's arms.
They share stories and play games
    never knowing
    that in another life
    their fathers might trade bullets
    instead of handshakes.

Their parents sit on opposite benches
    eyes meeting softly
    smiling tiredly
    weighted by parenthood
    but lifted by hope.

There are no uniforms to put on
    no strategies to form.
Only shared space
    and a field of Love
Holding the hands of their kids

instead of pistol grips.

In this revered place,
    there is no marching
    no fighting
    no rage.
Only children learning to live and play together
    and parents who can see
    that war was never the path to this place.
In order to get here, all must put down their arms,
    and forge a peaceful path forward together.

The Weight of Attack Ads

09/2024

They don't say my name, but I can hear it
    in their diatribes against my athletic sisters.
As if they can't possibly have
    achieved anything through effort.
As if my brothers don't also achieve athletic heights.
As if every child who doesn't fit neatly
    into their narrow lines is a threat.
They fashion weapons sharp and cold
    and aim them at children
    any child too soft, or too bold
    too much, too little
    too unique to be limited.
    by what they think boys and girls must be.

I feel the pain because when they erase these kids
    they sweep us all away
    anyone brave enough to be different.

They make us out to be wolves
    for the crimes of living,
    playing, breathing without fear.
They make our joy into a threat
    our very existence
    into a gruesome battle.
And I carry these wounds like an anchor on my chest.

I know it's not just an ad - it's a weapon.
Buried deep into the hearts of my brothers and sisters
Some will be scarred beyond repair
Their wound festering until it breaks open
    oozing and aching.
Until it's too much, and a child in pain,

in need of healing,
decides that this world is too cruel to live in.

I stand now as living proof,
    wounded but unbroken,
    and in this moment,
    a glimmer of hope shines through.
Someone sees me,
    not as a talking point,
    not as a vote to count,
    me, a person.
With skin, and breath, and a heart so full of love
    that I fear it may burst.

She says I deserve to play
To live and grow into the best version of myself.
Without the chains of an identity
    that I can never truly claim.
She says I deserve care,
    even if I were behind bars.
Because even in the darkest places
    our hearts beat, and we all yearn to become whole.

And I weep, for in a world where many wish to erase me
    there are forces holding them back,
    saying defiantly, "Let him stay."

But those fools take that kindness
    and morph it into a weapon too!
They call it weakness, failure.
As if supporting me is something shameful.
They bury my truth in shouted lies,
    but I can hear it,
    and I'll echo it with my every breath.

The weight is heavy,
    but I feel, deep down, a softening.
Because for once, someone is fighting for me.

In her eyes, I am not up for debate.
I am simply, beautifully, *alive*.

Bonus Points

10/2024

I was once at the bottom
Not from addiction or disease
    but from a deep hatred of myself
I wanted to be a normal kid so badly
    but I was the child of newcomers
    and my identity felt uncertain
    so I got picked on a lot
    and so many were so cruel
    I almost lost myself.

But after the storm, I got help.
They helped me with my anger,
    with my body image,
    with my adoption trauma.
    and I realized,
    I still felt the weight of it all
Because my inside didn't match my outside.
    so we found the right path,
    and I got the care I needed.

Now I'm feeling great,
    I wake up filled with purpose.
I've gone from despair to a revival of my spirit.
I love my life, my family, my community,
    and the goodness in this world.
    and I want to help as many people see it as I can
    before I finally go.
I'm lucky I'm here.

Everything from here is bonus points.

The Ones Who Show Up
10/2024

They show up
    when the world is broken.
When the floods rise high,
    and the winds strip the earth bare.
They stand in the mud, cold to the bone.
Giving freely their hours and Love.

They don't ask for thanks, or cash a check.
They hope to heal the broken places.
And yet, they are met with doubt,
    hardened hearts, and angry words.

They didn't have to come.
They have homes and families, too.
But they loved you so much that they came.
To lift weight and hearts.
To save what was left.
Only to be met
    with callous disregard
    with lies and slander.

If you wish, it is your right to criticize
    but know that
    the best among us
    are much too busy to listen.
Our sleeves are rolled
Our brows are sweaty
Our backs are tired
Our feet are weary.
If you really want us to listen,
    you'll have to come out with us.
For out here, we are working.
Out here, we are doing our best.
And we can't wait to see you give yours.

On Grief

10/2024

For a long time, I carried the names
    of my brother's killers in my wallet.
I'm not really sure why.
I know I hated them.
I blamed them.
I blamed you all for what they had done.
For years I held the rage deep in my chest and on my hip.
My shield and sword
Never realizing a shield can block the sun
    and swords only cut deeper.

I see now -
    I was unfair.
To turn my pain against the world.
Especially the Badge.
To allow my sorrow to twist into hatred.
For those who show up every day
    protecting and serving,
    doing their best.

You didn't deserve to be scorched
    by the wildfire burning in my heart.
You didn't pull the trigger.
You didn't take his breath.

I may never forgive the ones who did.
But I can ask for the forgiveness of the many who didn't.

I'm still learning how to heal these wounds.
I'm seeing the sameness between us now
We have the same values,
    we carry similar weights.
It's hard to help in a fearful world.
Where they see you first as the enemy.

Canvasser's Prayer

10/2024

Procedure:
Knock the door
Take one step back
Smile
Take a deep breath
Recite the following silently:

May you be happy.
May you be safe.
May you be free from suffering.
May you soon know peace.
May you be peaceful
should you choose to open the door.

Great work.
Now take a deep breath.
Count to 10.

If no answer,
    leave your literature in a place
    where the wind won't remove it.
Smile and wave.
Tell the home to have a nice day.
For you never know
    if a camera
    or a child
    may be watching
    and be moved to kindness.

Dear Voter
10/2024

We gather around you now, our voices stretching through time. You carry our hopes - what will you choose?

Jesus, who preached "Love thy neighbor," asks:
Does this leader practice love,
or spread fear?

Florence Nightingale, who healed with compassion and transformed care, whispers:
Does this leader care for the sick and vulnerable,
or do they ignore the suffering of those in need?

Clara Barton, who tended to wounded on battlefields, asks:
Does this leader rush to heal the wounded,
or do they leave the suffering behind in the chaos?

Jonas Salk, who gave the world a cure for polio, asks:
Does this leader believe in science,
or do they turn away from facts when they are needed most?

Abraham Lincoln, who held the Union together, reminds: A house divided cannot stand -
will this choice build,
or tear apart?

Eleanor Roosevelt, voice for human rights, asks:
Does this leader defend all,
or just a few?

Rosa Parks, who refused to give up her seat, whispers:
Does this candidate push for equality,
or leave some standing in the back?

Harriet Tubman, who led countless to freedom, asks:
Does this leader guide others toward liberty,
or do they close the door to those still in chains?

Ronald Reagan, who saw America as a shining city on a
hill, reminds: Does this leader welcome the tired and
poor,
or do they close the door on those who seek a better life?

The **boys of Bedford**, who gave everything on the shores
of Normandy, ask:
Does this leader honor our sacrifice,
or do they turn their back on the alliances we died to
protect?

The **victims of 9/11**, who died when terror struck our
shores, ask:
Does this leader unite us in our shared grief and hope,
or do they let fear and division tear us apart?

John Brown, who took up arms for the enslaved, calls
out: Does this leader stand against injustice,
or do they let the chains of hatred remain?

Chief Joseph, who fought for his people's right to live
on their lands, asks:
Does this leader respect the earth and its first people,
or do they take without care for what is sacred?

The **Tuskegee Airmen**, who fought fascism abroad and
racism at home, ask:
Does this leader see all men as equal,
or do they let prejudice cloud their judgment?

The **soldiers of Ukraine**, who laid down their lives to
protect their homes, ask:
Does this leader stand with those who fight for freedom,

or do they turn away, leaving the brave to fall alone?

We've seen what happens when leaders divide us with
fear.
So now, as you mark your choice, ask yourself:
Will this leader bring us together,
or leave us more divided than before?

America Builds the Best

10/2024

The captain's job is to push -
>to get the team to give everything,
>to leave it all on the field, no holding back.

And when it's close,
>so close that a recount or a replay
>could have made the difference,
>so could every yard, every inch, every door knock.

If we gave our best and came up short,
>we know we did all we could.
>That's what matters.

But if we spend too much time looking back at the last game,
>we're not getting ready for the next one.

And we'll lose again -
>because while we're busy blaming the refs,
>they're putting in reps, getting better.

It's not just about the trophy.

Yeah, we all want a fair game,
>but refs are human too.
>They'll make bad calls sometimes.
>That doesn't mean we tear down the whole league
>over one mistake.

Our performance isn't defined by the refs -
>it's defined by us.

We've got to ask:
>Did we leave it all on the line?

If the answer's yes, maybe we ask for a replay.
>But we respect the decision either way.

If the answer is no, then there's no point in blaming anybody
>but ourselves;
>we have to go out and put in the work.

That's the thing -
>there's always going to be someone better at something.

That's why we play the games.
That's why we want our opponents to get better too
because when we face the best,
it forces us to rise to the challenge.
They push us,
we push them,
and together, we raise the level of play.

If we want to be the best,
we have to build each other up,
so we both have a chance
to take down that big team from far away.

Losing to the best team? That's not failure.
We *want* the best team to win.
If we push them to play their best,
that's a victory too.
Their success is our success,
because it makes the whole game stronger.

Winning isn't just about who holds the trophy at the end.
It's about how we carry ourselves after the game,
how we come back stronger.
Because when we build each other up, we all get better.
And that's what makes America great:
America builds good winners.

Fingers Pointing At the Moon

These poems
Are imperfect
Some won't resonate
With every reader
Some may even
Prove controversial
But my enduring hope
Is that they may serve
As fingers which point to the moon.
Just as the writings I have read
Have served me.

So unto you, I close:
May you be happy.
May you be safe.
May you soon be free from suffering.
May you soon know your true nature.
May you soon feel belonging.

ABOUT THE AUTHOR

Luke Rouker is a poet, advocate, and devoted community member living in central Ohio. After moving frequently as a child, Luke found a lasting community in Southwest Virginia, spending much of his childhood in the Appalachian Mountains. He went on to earn his engineering degree at The Ohio State University and still cheers for the Buckeyes every Saturday in the fall. Luke draws inspiration from nature, social justice, and personal experiences of resilience and growth. When he's not writing, Luke works as a site reliability engineer, cycles in Pelotonia, volunteers with the Red Cross, and is active in political and community efforts. Luke's poetry reflects a commitment to love, equity, and the power of connection, shaped by Lutheran teachings, Buddhist practice, and a belief in radical compassion and Love.

This collection of poems represents a deeply personal journey, touching on themes of family, loss, identity, and hope. Luke is grateful to his wife, family, friends, and community for their constant support in bringing these words to life.